Miss Guided

Molefe Mohlamonyane

Independently Published: Molefe Mohlamonyane
1st Edition: 2021
Published in South Africa

The author has tried to trace and acknowledge sources/resources/individuals. Names and characters, places and incidents are purely fictional and bear no relationship to real-life individuals.If any images/information is incorrectly attributed or credited, the author is pleased to rectify these omissions at the earliest opportunity.

ISBN: 978-0-620-93102-1

Book Production Services:
Phetogo Book Publishers
0115075013/ 0606539238
info@phetogobookpublishers.co.za

Written by
Molefe Mohlamonyane
molefe@live.co.za
0824326420

Miss Guided

"A Pen is Mightier than the Sword"- Edward Bulwer-Lytton

Dedication

To God Almighty be the glory! It is through your mercy that I am where I am today; I am forever grateful. Thank you Father for guiding me, for the strength to continue every time reasons to give up became stronger, and for helping me to stand up after every fall.

I dedicate this book to my late father Morake, the perennial well of wisdom from which I drank with great enthusiasm. We did not know the value and quality of what you taught us at the time, but we do now look back at those lessons with a great sense of appreciation. You may have gone but your guidance, teachings and tutelage will continue to live for generations to come.

My mother Morongwa, a motivator and problem solver of note. Thank you mama for teaching us to appreciate the beauty in simplicity.

My siblings Mogapi, Moipone and Mmatsale, thank you for being by my side through and through even when you thought my ideas were way more than plain crazy. If I were to be afforded an opportunity to choose who I would want to have as siblings, I will without any doubt, choose you.

My cousin Lolo Ditshego, a shining light that helped us see where we should be going and not only where we wanted to go.

My wife Ntwana, my pillar of strength and great source of inspiration. I would not have managed to do a half of the things I have without your continued support. Thank you for always encouraging me to see possibilities instead of obstacles. I owe it all to you.

My children Mohapi, Tshiamo and Leago, you are the reason I look forward to every new day. This is one way to confirm that no matter how many times we fall we must make sure that we rise again after every fall.

PREFACE

The assumption that once young people have completed their tertiary studies they will get jobs and break the cycle of poverty in their families seems to be misplaced. Our focus is on those who are fortunate to get into the job market after graduating.

It is critical for our youth to be taught how to make better decisions about money. This will help them deal with the issues of poverty which keeps them financially unstable as a result of debt, family responsibilities and pressure to succeed. Societal expectations add to the challenges young graduates have to navigate so that they can be classified as being successful.

Student Brands reported as its research outcomes from a study they conducted in 2015 that South African students' six most common spending categories were entertainment, clothing, education, accommodation and travel. Pressure from society tends to blind most youth as it comes disguised as affirmation and recognition. Most people do the unimaginable in order to impress those around them. Conforming to societal expectations and demands is one of the most dangerous habits modern man has developed. Dave Ramsey summed it up well in his quote when he said that: "We buy things we don't need with money we don't have to impress people we don't like."

This book reveals the challenges faced by young professionals in their quest to live up to societal expectations. I am confident that most readers will relate to some aspects of the journey travelled by Molemo and his family. Hopefully your exposure to this family will:

Inspire you not to succumb to these pressures and be as true to yourself as possible. Create an awareness of the importance of making good decisions about money. Encourage you to be deliberate in breaking the cycle of poverty. Build your resilience in dealing with multiple obstacles you are bound to come across.

Rise young lions rise and reclaim your rightful status in society. Lead through authenticity. 'Be yourselves, everyone else is taken.' Oscar Wilde

Table of Contents

CHAPTER 1

"To Be Yourself in A World That Is Constantly Trying To Make You Something Else Is the Greatest Accomplishment" -Ralph Waldo Emerson

Growing up in the dusty yet vibrant streets of Mamelodi was a fun filled affair. Weekdays were characterised by thick clouds of smoke rising from the coal stoves and braziers used to boil water to get learners and workers ready for the new day as well as the mama's who got magwinya ready for those on their way to school and work. Taxi drivers hooting for attention to ferry both young and old to their various destinations. It is business as usual as everyone goes through their paces to earn a living.

Even those hoping for a change in fortunes are up and about getting ready to knock on the doors of potential employers. I admire their resilience and commitment. They are not deterred by the number of dead ends they reach with the passing of each and every day. They go to bed disappointed that the day did not yield what they had anticipated but wake up the next day with renewed hope.

Weekends on the other hand were characterised by sounds of various genres of music belting from speakers placed on stoeps of most of the houses in a street as if each of the households is trying to show off whose music system could produce the clearest and loudest sound or who had the most potent music collection. I should be forgiven for concluding that whoever coined the phrase; 'Mamelodi bly duma' was inspired by the passion displayed by mostly ma Grootman who played the music as well as the sounds produced by their Kenwood, TEAC, Technics, Marantz and Pioneer speakers.

Equally interesting is the lingua franca used by ma 'Grootman and Susters'. A cocktail of languages which requires thorough practice and one's full attention or else 'O ka se verstane fokol my authi ke a o bethela loosely translated 'you won't understand a thing my brother, I am telling you'. It somehow displayed the essence of their being in the township through shaping and embracing sePitori (the language of the Pretorians).

It was in this very dusty yet vibrant township where Molemo was born 27 years ago, coming from very humble beginnings. Both his parents were like many other in the township, general workers in the surrounding suburbs of Pretoria. They earned meagre incomes enough to allow them to live on the breadline. Despite their low earnings Molemo's parents wanted the best for him and his three younger siblings. The general community's levels of education including that of Molemo's parents were enough to enable them to read and write their names and surnames thus placing a huge responsibility on the few who went further up the rungs of the ladder education has turned into. It was therefore a usual sight for parents to knock on doors of those in the know so that their children could be helped with the completion of their school work. I have a vivid memory of Molemo explaining the joy he derived the day he found out that the Sepedi word 'mokitlana' meant credit.

He said that he was frustrated not knowing where to turn to for help and when he came across the elderly Koko Mma Mogadime, a highly respected member of the community, he complained about how unfair their Sepedi teacher was. When the wise, old lady enquired why he felt the teacher was unfair, he immediately informed Koko that he has searched everywhere he could for the Sepedi translation of the word credit and thus far his efforts drew a blank.

He thought that there was no way he would find an answer as such a word does not exist in Sepedi otherwise someone would have already come to his rescue. His other thought which left Koko in stitches was that the word did not exist as credit was not a Sepedi concept. Koko had a very good laugh on hearing the reasons for the complaint and with a sense of reassurance informed Molemo that the answer he was looking for is mokitlana. It was only then that the adage, ‘it takes a village to raise a child’ reverberated in Molemo’s head.

Though an answer was provided and the homework on the verge of completion, Koko took the liberty to educate Molemo about the traditional African practice based on what has become known in modern day as the concept Ubuntu - Botho. Bapedi say ‘motho ke motho ka batho’. One could interpret the statement to mean 'I am therefore you are'. It refers to having a deep sense of another person's humanity.

How to demonstrate being a human being to another human being. It requires people to be more outwardly focused instead of inwardly. It reflects the significance of people moving towards each other and not drifting apart and being alone. It reminds me of Martin Luther King Junior's quote that; "In a real sense, all life is inter-related. All men are caught in an inescapable network of mutuality, tied in a single garment of destiny. Whatever affects one directly, affects all indirectly. I can never be what I ought to be until you are what you ought to be, and you can never be what you ought to be until I am what I ought to be… this is the inter-related structure of reality."

She fondly spoke about her experiences as she grew up in her rural Limpopo village of Ga-Mphahlele. She said that whenever a person or a family would arrive in their community expressing their intention to assume residence in the village, they would be welcomed with both hands. They would be allocated a piece of land to erect a structure in which they would reside, a piece of land on which they would cultivate crops as well as a cow referred to as 'kgomo ya mafiša'. These served as a provision of a lifeline towards ensuring accumulation of wealth and an opportunity for the affected individuals and or families to live independently.

The person allocated the cow(s) would look after them and whenever they would reproduce, he would keep the offspring as his. This meant that the more care you give to the animals, the faster you would amass your own wealth. Mind you in most African nations, families who had a lot of livestock were highly respected and regarded as very rich. There was a realisation that for communities to thrive it was important for them to sustain the assistance they would extend to those in need and avoid creation and entrenchment of a dependency syndrome. Those who benefited from this Ubuntu programme would often extend a helping hand to others in similar situations they experienced.

The poverty that continues to stare at us was unknown during those times for the following reasons:

Members of the community were willing to lend a hand in the upliftment of their fellow men. They were not too proud to admit that they needed assistance. They were not shy to ask for such assistance. Getting assistance was perceived as a lifeline meant to get a person back on their feet and not a creation of dependency. Western influence of individualism which replaced 'we' with 'I' has eroded the fabric of ubuntu – botho. The respect afforded people based on their common humanity has been replaced by the wealth accumulation and 'improvement' of one's social standing.

Molemo continued to admire Koko's wisdom and understood why members of this community were helping each other from time to time. He hoped that he would one day make a mark as an upstanding member of society. He believed that he did not have to wait until he had completed his studies or when he was older to contribute towards improving the lives of those around him. He had a very enquiring mind and strived to find answers to the questions that crossed his mind from time to time. He spent many afternoons at the local library doing research on the internet and scores of encyclopedias at his disposal. Whenever an answer evaded him he would approach knowledgeable members of society starting with his own parents. He realised that though his parents did not have formal school qualifications, they had a wealth of knowledge and wisdom accumulated from the most important university called life. This he called real education which in his view differed from certification. He saw the collection of certificates, diplomas and degrees which was not accompanied by the ability to make a positive contribution towards the betterment of society as fruitless.

Molemo was happy as he hurried home to do the final touches to his school work which was due for submission the following day. His English teacher, Mrs. Mabapa observed his ability to argue factually and introduced him to the debating society. He became an instant hit despite being the youngest member of the debating team being the only learner in grade 8 to be accepted into this 'elite' league. There were fireworks when he first represented the schools' debating team in a contest with the mighty Lekoa Shandu High School in the Vaal Triangle township of Sharpeville. The adjudicators marveled at the genius displayed by this rough diamond and were unanimous in awarding him with the Speaker of the Day prize. His team heaped him with praises as they acknowledged the abundant knowledge of current affairs he possessed, his agility, versatility, and ability to think on his feet.

He remained level headed and worked even harder as he prepared for the next contests. It came as no surprise that his team topped the charts in Pretoria and later became part of the top ten debating teams in Gauteng. They may not have had the twang to attract attention, but they would without a doubt draw attention with their posture, confidence and ability to present factually accurate arguments. I wonder how they would have fared had the contests been conducted nationally. I am confident that they would have given a lot of high profile high schools a run for their money.

The hunger they displayed was a direct translation of the commitment, interest, passion, diligence and work ethic of most teachers at their school. They made every effort to contribute towards the success of their charges despite the limited resources at their disposal. As a sign of their dedication they inter alia, conducted morning and afternoon studies for all grades from Monday to Thursday without fail. The 24-hour turnaround time for the marking of assessment tasks was further indication of the teachers' awareness of the enormity of the task at hand and their ability to fulfil it with great aplomb. Their actions stood true to the identification of teaching as a labour of love and a calling. As profoundly expressed by the renowned American lawyer and politician, Brad Henry; "A good teacher can inspire hope, ignite the imagination, and instil a love for learning".

How I wish that teachers like these were celebrated by their respective communities in appreciation of the wonderful job they continue to do. Sadly, the value of the teaching profession has been reduced to one of the unimportant careers in more ways than one. The meagre salaries earned by teachers has a negative impact on luring gifted youngsters to the profession. The salaries offered in a particular career seems to be the indication of how important that career or profession is.

Hopefully the status quo will change sooner before further damage is done to this noble profession. Molemo continued to grow from strength to strength as he became the key contributor towards the good grades his younger siblings obtained. He was selfless as he extended his services beyond his home. His siblings' peers would often be seen at his house with their school books so that he could help them with the completion of the tasks they were given. He was an industrious learner and soon some of the few affluent and respected members of the community heard about his academic prowess. They enlisted his services to help their children with their school work. For his efforts, they gave him gifts in the form of cash, clothes, books and edibles. Whatever they saw fit to offer him they insisted that he has it no matter how much he tried to reject the offerings. He helped his fellow man out of the goodness of his heart acknowledging just how important it was to pay it forward. The teachings of Koko Mma Mogadime inspired his actions.

He accepted the gifts with great reluctance but went on to share them with his siblings. He was however very stingy with money or should I say careful on what he spent it on? He put away his money with the view to use it one day when it has accumulated sufficiently to pay for soccer boots, socks, shirt and pants. Getting a tracksuit would be a bonus he thought. Three months later he had not only bought himself all he had wished for but also a soccer ball for his siblings. They were very grateful to have such a responsible and generous older brother. His parents were equally proud of him and expressed their gratitude for his contribution. It would have taken them ages to be able to provide him with the things he had bought himself. Money was very tight and therefore every cent counted. It would have been a blessing to have multiple Molemos who would drive and support the education of the young people in the community. It is the only way in which the community can develop and live beyond the breadline. The current reality of young people admiring and striving to emulate negative role models would be a thing of the past.

The other day I was in a taxi to town. The bubbly taxi driver apologised that he had taken his sound system in for repairs otherwise he would be playing his popular music. It was as though his apology was an indication to the three young boys to start their discussion about how they admired Bra Ngamla. Ngamla is a local big shot who owns a fleet of elegant cars and a double storey house. His dress code is quite unique and classy. He is one of the revered members of the Mamelodi community. While his fleet of cars and dress code are signs of opulence, he has never worked for a day. Neither has he exchanged services or goods in return for money in any way possible. Those who claim to have closer relationships with him say that he is unapologetic about 'repossessing' what is 'rightfully' his which was forcefully taken from his ancestors. He is said to be a hardcore criminal who stole without limits. There was nothing too small or too big for him to steal. He was beyond kleptomania based on what they say.

The young men were expressing how they would love to follow in Ngamla's dodgy footsteps. They tried very hard to explain how useless school was and a complete waste of their precious time. Why one would work for an entire month and get paid only once, they asked. One must get money every day because he works every day and therefore instead of getting an education in order to get a good paying job was not their most preferred way to spend their time. They preferred to ‘phanda’ ahead of going the usual route taken by many community members.’Phanda’ is a term coined by the locals which refers to making money using whatever means possible. Whether it is through selling goods or rendering services but in this case the young men were referring to ‘earning’ their living through stealing from others. Their justification was that it was okay to take from the rich as they have plenty and would not be disadvantaged by what is taken from them. The rich have insured everything they own so there would be no harm taking from them they said.

I listened to their conversation with great concern disguised as keen interest and wondered what the reason was for these kinds of thoughts to be so entrenched in the minds of our youth. Even more concerning was the possibility of the mindset being a way of life for a greater percentage of the young people especially those growing up in townships. If it were to be confirmed that most young people believe in this view, then it would suggest that we will continue to be disadvantaged as the Black nation. The truth is that contrary to popular belief we are still disadvantaged and not previously disadvantaged as a lot of commentators declare.

Where does this kind of reasoning place us as a nation in relation to other nations of the world? Have we lost the plot as a people? It seems all well and good when people like the ‘highly revered’ are perceived to be living the lavish life. Splashing cash on cars, sipping very expensive whisky, smoking Cuban cigars, wearing trendy imported labels and frequent overseas trips is unfortunately not sustainable. Criminal activity cannot continue forever, it comes to an abrupt stop at some point and often with dire consequences.

There is however, still hope for our young people's mindsets can be learnt and adopted. It is incumbent upon us all to play an active role in determining the future of our children and nation collectively. We must inculcate a growth mindset in our youth to ensure that they spot gaps and provide solutions required by their society. There is no future for a dependency syndrome by living off handouts and thinking that when you are born into a not so affluent family, you are doomed. There is no opportunity to change the situation. Where you come from should not define who you are, it should instead inspire you to strive towards attaining your goals with greater determination. It is imperative that we remind ourselves of the advice to young people by the first democratically elected president of our great nation, South Africa, Nelson Mandela that;

"Education is the great engine of personal development. It is through education that the daughter of a peasant can become a doctor, that the son of a mineworker can become the head of the mine, which a child of farm workers can become the president of a great nation. It is what we make out of what we have, not what we are given, that separates one person from another."

CHAPTER 2

"Challenges Are What Makes Life Interesting And Overcoming Them Makes Life Meaningful"
–Anonymous

Bra Moss was sitting leisurely at his favourite water hole exchanging pleasantries of how great the day was. He had a habit of starting off with his Zamalek quarts and upgrade his imbibition to something stronger. White spirits like cane and vodka were his drinks of preference. He had just ordered his second nip suddenly it appeared as if something was amiss. He took a sip and then another before he sought a second opinion from his drinking buddy. 'My friend, something is not right here or am I drunk? This booze tastes nothing like the strong waters of mortality I am used to. Tears of queen Elizabeth, saliva of King George, I mean the real waters in which no fish can survive. Have a taste and tell me what you think. Are we taken for a ride my friend this is plain water, what do you think?'

Bra Steve also known as Stevovo took a sip, waited a bit as though confused, took another sip and another. He paused for a while and went seemed to be deep in thought. He took another sip then a gulp. 'Mngani wam siyadelelwa lana ekhaya, amanzi wodwa lawa', said bra Steve eventually in response to the question posed by his friend bra Moss. Loosely translated he meant that 'we are taken for a ride my friend this is just water'. I knew it, I knew it my friend. I know my poison so well no one can take me for granted. Bra Moss could not contain his anger and started shouting. Emma! Emma come here, what are you trying to do? I always thought very highly of you but this! How could you? How could you sell me water? This is the lowest anybody could go to no matter how desperate you are for money. Aikhona! Emma! He shouted some more. Nee man, ons is nie moegoes nie (no man, we are not stupid).

Bra Moss was a regular at Molemo's home where his mom Emma is trying out life as an emerging shebeen queen. She buys a few beverages ranging from beer quarts, spirits and ciders. Because her clientele does not imbibe a lot especially during the week, she decided to decant the spirits into nips and half jacks. Bra Moss' shouting went beyond the decibels Molemo's father could stomach. Before everyone knew it, he was out of his bedroom wielding a sjambok. Suddenly everyone one was on their feet making sure that the temperamental Bra Chris' wrath does not befall them. He was under normal circumstances, a reasonably peaceful man but could get quite nasty when his buttons were pushed. He believed that people would take advantage of situations especially after having a few intoxicating beverages and the sjambok was, according to him, the best language of communication in such circumstances.

In a few seconds bra Moss and Stevovo were apologising saying there was nothing wrong with the drink it was instead their erratic taste buds which caused all this unnecessary furore. Seeds of doubt were now sown in their minds, were their beverages tampered with or was it an error of judgement on their part?

The next day Bra Moss and Stevovo were back at their water hole sipping on their favourite drinks. They had asked for an opportunity to meet Bra Chris and Emma to express how sorry they were to have doubted their integrity. In my honest view this was more like a situation where someone steps on you and instead of you alerting them about their infringement you apologise to them stating that your foot found itself under theirs by mistake. You would even vow that you would make sure this does not happen again. Ga bo lefšega a go lliwe they say.

Molemo continued achieving success after success through inter alia his hunger and determination. He was admired by peers and adults alike for the drive and passion he displayed when doing all he did. The notion that success breeds success seemed to have been confirmed to be the gospel truth. Contrary to general assumption, Molemo's success did not have any connection with his general behaviour. He was not one to stick to the straight and narrow. He had become a magnet to challenges. Like many boys his age, he tried almost everything from cigarettes, benzine, dagga and an array of alcoholic beverages. The biggest mistake he could make was for his actions to be discovered by his strict parents Chris and Emma. If any of them were to find out he would be in huge trouble.

That most of Molemo's peers in the same grade were way older than him added fuel to the fire. His companions in the debating and other societies were also older. This difference in age meant difference in experiences which affected the quality of their discussions. At times they would discuss how vibrant the situation was at a party or stokvel they had attended and he would not have anything to contribute towards that discussion. Other times it would be about their boy and girl friends and this too was at that stage untrampled territory for Molemo. He desperately wanted to be part of this cool crew and had to think about something he could do so that he could be accepted. He resorted to spending as much time as he could with his older peers and do as many things they did as he possibly could.

He was however still not fully accepted into most of the situations enjoyed by his older peers. He had to provide some sort of 'admission fee' ranging from alcoholic beverages, cigarettes and food. He used his earnings from the extra lessons he offered and when these funds were depleted he would tap from the limited domestic resources. He would from time to time dilute the spirits (gin and vodka) with water and take a nip or two to his friends. When his mom was away he would sneak a quart or two into his school bag and take these to school. This in his view was a sign of maturity, proving that he was way more mature than his tiny frame. 'It is better to walk alone than with a crowd going in a wrong direction. Do what you feel is right.' Anonymous.

In Emma and Chris' eyes it was sheer madness for Bra Moss and Stevovo to make the ridiculous claims of their drinks being tampered with. The same is unfortunately not the case to you and I who have been made aware of the extent to which our beloved Molemo would go in seeking recognition and acceptance by his older peers. We know that there could have been some truth in the claims of an inferior quality of the drinks they were served and that they had every right to complain. The seemingly negligible actions of this young man had the potential to spiral into something unfathomable. The budding family business could have easily been brought to its knees with patrons crying foul because of the quality of beverages served. The defensive nature of Molemo's dad was not helpful either as he threatened those who complained with violence. Lawyers costs could have been required and possibly jail terms here and there if anyone had responded differently.

I have learnt that it is important for people who render services of whatever kind to seek feedback from those they serve so as to determine the quality of their offering. In this way one is able to keep his clients happy and attract new ones. If you do things the way you always have without keeping abreast with developments in your field you run the risk of offering below par service thereby alienating your clientele. As the quote attributed to author, speaker, management expert and business consultant Ken Blanchard goes, 'Feedback is the breakfast of champions'.

It is surprising just how lucky Molemo was, it was somewhat inexplicable how he was let off the hook when everything else suggested he should take the brunt for his actions. Only the other day a teacher walked into the classroom he was sitting in together with his older mates. The smell of alcohol and the unusually loud episodes of laughter screamed for the teacher's attention and he obliged. The boys were shaking like leaves at the sight of the teacher, Mr. Ngobeni who was a disciplinarian of note. Only then did they realise how stupid they were to imbibe the intoxicating waters on the school premises especially in a classroom. That it was a normal school day made matters even more difficult.

Mr. Ngobeni was irritated and disgusted by the behaviour of these young people but managed to keep his calm. He ordered all the younger looking learners out of the classroom as he wanted to deal with the real culprits. It was surprising that the key contributor to the imbibition was let off the hook that easily as it was somewhat unthinkable that someone so tiny and yet so productive would be part of something so destructive. He would exercise better judgement and not engage in these vile activities thought Mr. Ngobeni. Little did he know that it was Molemo who brought the alcoholic beverages to school. He put a nip of vodka, gin and three quarts of beer in his sports bag. He left the house without anyone noticing anything amiss and made it to school. The need to belong turned him into something else. Uncanny, extremely cunning with execution way beyond military in precision. He remained the child they all knew and admired at home and in the neighbourhood.

One of the community's blue–eyed boys, the envy of many a parent. It must however be shared that most of the children in his neighbourhood did not like him particularly because their parents would mention Molemo's name whenever they went astray. They were always advised in not so polite ways to take a leaf from Molemo's book. They did not take kindly to this and it created some unnecessary beef towards him. The older guys were summoned to the Headmaster's office to account for their deeds or is it misdeeds? Due to the seriousness of their transgression, their parents had to be called in for a formal disciplinary process. They knew how serious this was as they could be suspended for a week or even worse, be expelled from school. The prospects of the bright futures they saw in front of them gradually flying out of that proverbial window. Dire as the situation seemed, the young men decided to keep things as they were and vowed never to mention Molemo's involvement in this whole saga. Let him be seen with the lens the community has chosen to see him, exposing him would be more detrimental than retaining the high hopes the elders hold of and in him.

The boys survived expulsion and suspension primarily because they were first 'time offenders' and that they were remorseful about their shameful actions. They were not necessarily first-time offenders as they had consumed alcoholic beverages on the school premises a significant number of times before they were caught. I have seen them do it repeatedly and can vouch for that with greater confidence. Many in the school community were not pleased with the outcome of the disciplinary process and the most vociferous of the parents were Molemo's parents as they cited that this unruly behaviour would adversely influence their son and his siblings' behaviour if it is not sufficiently addressed. If and only if they knew the force behind the misdemeanor. Despite the school community's feelings about the ruling, sanity returned, and the decision of the disciplinary committee was respected. Molemo was again let off the hook. Ever heard about surviving through the skin of your teeth? Methinks this is a perfect example of such. It was sheer luck and nothing of his making, he had no reason to claim otherwise.

Chapter 3

"The only time success comes before work is in the dictionary" -Harvey Specter

"There is no way we are going to match the pass rate we achieved at the end of last year unless we do something drastically different. "Learners are doing as they please since this nonsense about Student Representative Councils began. "They literally spend only a day or two in class per week and the rest in the streets involved in all sorts of mischief." These were the strong views expressed by the Principal of J Kekana High School, Mr. S Motale where Molemo attended.

Even though Mr. Motale challenged the actions of the students, he was a well-known activist who spent time behind bars as a result of his participation in the struggle for the liberation of Africans. He tried everything to hide this side of his. It is however unclear whether this was because of the stern warnings and beatings he is alleged to have received during those trying times or whether it was due to his decision not to let the students exploit his struggle credentials and start disrespecting his authority.

It all started with what seemed like a protest over school uniform at the school, but it ended up taking a completely new direction. One Friday morning, the Principal conducted random uniform checks and all the learners whose uniform was not compliant were ordered to go home and return with proper uniform. What was confusing to some was that they had grey pants and white shirts as required but they were told that their shade of grey was not acceptable.

This unfortunate occurrence ignited the learners' consciousness about the struggles the black child had to go through, some of these were not only unjust but plain unnecessary as well. It is suspected that this was one of the incidents that triggered student activism during that time which halted teaching and learning in Pretoria. Mobilisation of students began in earnest and continued at a pace no one had anticipated. Learners went beyond the obvious challenges of school uniform and this time demanded free and compulsory education and the complete eradication of Bantu Education. The authorities would have none of it leading to detention of student leaders for extended periods of time. Some paid the supreme sacrifice through the bullet of the oppressor and other vile means. Others were maimed physically and the signs of their years of battling are there for everyone to see. The most painful were the emotional scars emanating from the incidents of torture endured by these young activists.

The level of preparedness of those in authority to listen to the cries of the students was non-existent. It was without doubt a just cause they were fighting but unfortunately the regime of that time was not prepared to give in to the students' demands. The nature and extent of the student struggle and the resistance it was met with is a discussion for another day. It requires a special mention as part of the rich History of events which unfolded in these dusty streets of Mamelodi and the surrounding townships. On a lighter note, I am told that one teacher, Mr. Ngobeni was faced with a mammoth task of providing updates on the situation at the school including the actual demands posed by the 'unruly' students whenever he met this seemingly interested member of the community. It was the retired Postman, Ntate Maringa. He would ask 'what the learners did today?' and upon receiving an update add his two cents' worth of views on whatever matter the teacher had shared with him.

After months of uncertainty the schools resumed their normal operation. Some concessions were made in the interest of empowering learners educationally. The struggle would continue but this time around while attending school. They felt very strongly that the time lost by learners may contribute adversely towards their academic performance. Catch up plans were in motion and learners showed greater determination to work with their educators. They attended the extra classes organised to help them catch up with aspects of the syllabus they have missed during the time they were protesting with such vigour you could have easily sworn that their lives depended on the lessons. They had no intention to taint the impeccable record of the grade 12 predecessors.

One Saturday afternoon after the catch-up lessons Mr. Ngobeni met the retired Postman Mr. Maringa who asked what the learners had done on this day. Mr. Ngobeni immediately told him about the learners' response when they were asked, 'who killed Julius Caesar?' None of them raised their hands to respond to the question and when the teacher insisted that they do each of them said they did not know. Mr. Maringa burst into laughter and said, "These naughty children! They know who killed him but do not want to expose the culprit who did this evil act. It is without a doubt one of them, these little crooks! Call in the cops and they will tell them who was responsible!" Mr. Ngobeni left in a huff without saying a word seemingly afraid to burst into his signature rapturous laughter which could offend Mr. Maringa. Clearly, Mr. Maringa was unaware of the Shakespearean gem penned during the Elizabethan era titled Julius Caesar.

I am reminded of the warning attributed to Alexander Pope in his essay 'an essay on criticism – when he said: "A little learning is a dangerous thing; drink deep or taste not the Pieran spring: there shallow draughts intoxicate the brain and drinking largely sobers us again." Whenever we are not sure of what is shared with us, we better ask for clarity or go seek it elsewhere before we expose our shallow or non-existent understanding of the subject(s) under discussion.

Molemo and his peers were so focused on their school work to a point that they were no longer attending their soccer practices or any other form of socialisation. It was books, books and more books all day every day. He had to find a gap on Sundays for church as his parents never allowed any of their charges to miss church. They even threatened anyone who would question their religious ways and their demand for everyone to attend church every Sunday with immediate removal from their homestead. It was their rules and anybody who felt they were unable or unwilling to comply should find themselves alternative accommodation. That all the children were now tired of challenging the rules and complied without fail. A rare opportunity for socialisation presented itself in the form of a school sports and debate challenge from Mbilwi High School in Limpopo. Learners were excited and grabbed this opportunity with both hands. Molemo was amongst the first to pay for the outing. In the evening of the Friday before the trip he packed his 'Padkos' (food supplies for the trip) and went to bed early. All the usual stuff carried by learners were in his bag. The choice assorted biscuits, chocolate slab, big packet of potato chips, big cans of fish, baked beans and spaghetti, a loaf of bread, a tub of yoghurt and four cans of fizzy soft drinks.

The older learners would sneak into their bags an assortment of alcoholic beverages. These were often 'sniffed out' by educators. It spelled a lot of trouble for those whose beverages were sniffed out and confiscated. They would have to face the music when school resumed the following Monday. This, however, did not stop them from bringing with them the forbidden drinks.

Molemo hardly slept on Friday night as he was awoken several times by the anxiety of being left behind as he feared that he would over sleep. The children accompanied by six educators hit the road in four fully packed buses headed for the Limpopo Province. Three hours or so later, they were walking jovially on the premises of Mbilwi High School.

They were received with ample warmth and most of them were intent on creating longer lasting relations with some of their peers at the host school. Molemo had vowed to wow one of the most beautiful girls at Mbilwi and return with their postal address, a telephone number would be a bonus he thought.

It is surprising that during that time there were limited telephones across the country and most people relied on centralised public telephones yet very few people were late for their appointments or missed them. Today almost everyone has an individualised mobile phone or direct access to a landline and yet punctuality and or honouring of appointments remain thorny hindrances. Difficult as it may be to locate the actual reasons for the occurrence of these hindrances one cannot help it but to lay the blame on the doorstep of the following possibilities:

The limited access made people to honour their appointments as future access to means of communication was not guaranteed. People valued their relationships more during those times as compared to today. There were limitations in terms of the ability to interact with multiple individuals at a time. There were of course exceptions to the rule as is the case with all other situations. Virtual connectedness has taken over the need and value of face to face meetings. If I were to miss an appointment with you I can be able to connect with you within a reasonable period through a variety of media.

We spend far too much on communication platforms and connect very little with those who are less than a stone throw away from us. We spend time sharing views with friends in faraway places while we fail to have meaningful discussions with those sitting around the dinner table with us.

His Holiness the Dalai Lama's Paradox of our times sums up our current reality:

The Paradox of Our Times

Is that we have taller buildings, but shorter tempers
Wider freeways, but narrower viewpoints
We spend more, but we have less.
We have bigger houses, but smaller families
More conveniences, but less time.
We have more degrees, but less sense
More knowledge, but less judgement
More experts, but more problems
More medicines, but less wellness.
We have multiplied our possessions but reduced our values.
We talk too much, love too seldom, and hate too often
We have learnt how to make a living, but not a life.
We have added years to life, but not life to years.
We've been all the way to the moon and back
But have trouble crossing the street to meet the new neighbours.
We have conquered outer space, but not inner space.
We've cleaned up the air but polluted our soul.
We've split the atom, but not our prejudice.
We've higher incomes, but lower morals.
We've become long on quantity but short on quality.
These are the times of tall men, and short character;
Steep profits, and shallow relationships.
These are the times of world peace, but domestic warfare,
More leisure, but less fun; more kinds of food, but less nutrition.
These are the days of two incomes, but more divorces;
Of fancier houses, but broken homes.

It is a time when there is much in the show window, and nothing in the stockroom.
A time when technology can bring this letter to you,
And a time when you can choose,
Either to make a difference.... or just hit, delete.

Having pointed a finger at the above, I still believe there is a need for us to explore the real reasons behind this reality and find ways and means to remedy the situation. A young man or woman who did not return from a school outing such as this one with an address to which he would send his letters expressing sweet little nothings was perceived as a failure. Post outing discussions often centred on boasting about the names and addresses of their 'newly found loves'. Receipt of a reply to a letter one had sent out to their 'newly found lover' reciprocating the declaration of their undying love presented the recipients with bragging rights. Inclusion of a photograph or two of the 'lover' cemented the need for the recipient to be treated with enormous respect by his peers.

The benefits which came with these accolades created some unfortunate unintended consequences. Bakang, Molemo's bosom friend religiously received letters from all the girls he had met during school outings. Their circle of friends envied and respected him greatly. Their envy and respect was eroded the day he lost his examination pad. The person who found the examination pad thought it best to hand it to one of Bakang's friends so that he could give it to him when the two met. The friend's curiosity on the other hand pushed him to open the examination pad and to his utter surprise, he found several letters Bakang had written to himself as though they came from different addresses and suitors. He could not wait to expose his discovery to all and sundry who admired Bakang albeit for seemingly all the wrong reasons.

It was until this time that they started to question the authenticity of his claims. Members of his inner circle suddenly remembered the cousins whose photographs were often shared with them under the pretext that they were Bakang's 'lovers' from the different school outings they had. This discovery nearly destroyed Bakang through alienation as the distance away from his friends made him to challenge his self-worth and general outlook on life. His ego was deflated to the lowest level possible. He missed school for a week sighting unwellness from an 'unknown bug' he caught. This 'unknown bug' devoured his appetite and eagerness to play outside.

He was however extremely fortunate that when his mother spotted his change in behaviour, he was open with her about the source of his 'illness', displeasure and grief. After five sessions with the local Psychologist he was almost back to his usual self. He says that the key lessons he learnt from this whole experience were: Never to allow yourself to be swayed by the desire for others' approval or fit in. Dr Seuss put it beautifully when he asked, "Why fit in when you were born to stand out?"

Key Lessons Learnt from Bakang's Experience Include:

It is very important that we never hide who we are or become someone we are not. We should learn to care more about who we really are than who anyone else wants us to be, and we need to discover our self-worth and embrace ourselves as we are. The value of being your authentic self can never be sufficiently emphasised. You do not have to seek validation from others to be authentic, instead strive to be who you truly are and be embraced or rejected for being yourself. Heed John Mason's warning when he said; "You were born original, don't die a copy."

Without really noticing, I have digressed significantly from what I wanted to share with you. During the visit to Limpopo, Molemo displayed his expertise both on the field of play as a goal minder for the school's senior team keeping a clean sheet. I am sure that had it not been for his heroics, the senior team would have conceded an avalanche of goals. It was surprising that the odd goal they scored salvaged J. Kekana's victory. As if that was not enough, he represented his debating team extremely well as the last speaker on the negative side. He went beyond paralysing the opposition and summing up the views of his side but also provided real practical solutions to the challenges expressed in the topic for debate.

He became an instant hit with peers from Gauteng and Limpopo alike. He was the pride of his school and the envy of those who experienced his prowess for the first time. He was confident that he was going to amass quite several addresses and telephone numbers from the wonderful ladies he has seen for the greater part of the day.

Once done with the debating contest, Molemo went outside to venture onto his next expedition. He almost fell from the radiance of the African queen he saw. A paragon of perfection, beauty at its best. It was as if the word 'most beautiful' was coined just after others saw her because neither the words beautiful and more beautiful were not adequate descriptors for this kind of enchantress. For a moment he stood there in great admiration deserted by speech. The eloquence he displayed inside the hall earlier on had evaporated into thin air. She was a paragon of perfection, beauty personified and an ambassador of vivacity.

Molemo regained consciousness and vowed to lure the beautiful lady his way. He mumbled a few words in Sesotho before realising that he was in fact in a different territory and had to change the medium of communication. He immediately defaulted to English and received a smile or two from the lady. He was frustrated when the lady's responses came in Xitsonga, a language he could not understand at all. He tried his best to entice the young lady to shift into the Queen's language, but his attempts fell flat. Defeated he left the lady and went to sit in the bus alone trying to figure out how he could have turned the opportunity he had earlier with the young lady into an address exchanging reality.

He was not the type to give up and he gathered strength and restarted his adventure. Discussions commenced very well but took a similar twist as the first one at the critical moment with language being the major hindrance. All signs indicated positive feedback and acceptance of his proposal, but it remained impossible for him to confirm what he thought was happening. He left Limpopo empty handed and vowed from that moment that he will make every effort to learn to speak as many languages as he possibly could. It is therefore not surprising that he eloquently communicates in nine of the 11 official South African languages. He is still learning to master Tshivenda and Siswati at this juncture. It makes perfect sense for one to extend their interests beyond the language users and go on to learn their language and cultures as well. This to me is a sign of respect. May we learn from the words of the first South African democratic President Nelson Mandela when he said; "If you talk to a man in a language he understands, that goes to his head. If you talk to him in his language that goes to his heart".

CHAPTER 4

"It's Not What You Are That Holds You Back, It's What You Think You Are Not." -Denis Waitley

Molemo's industrious high school career continued unhindered and as was expected he graced the front pages of the local and provincial newspapers having attained seven distinctions. It was quite a rare feat especially for learners attending local public schools with limited or no resources. It is again a reflection of what the learners and teachers had put in. The teachers worked on the learners' self-image and entrenched in each of them enormous self-belief which ensured that they gave their all in everything they did.

Success breeds success and you can never go wrong making a habit of meeting and exceeding the goals you set for yourself. It is very unfortunate that our society tends to overlook the contribution of the teachers when learners do well and apportion all blame on the teachers when learners do not do as well as expected. It is equally concerning that most of us fail to achieve greatness simply because we do not think that we have what it takes to do so. We think that greatness is foreign to us and can possibly only attained by some people elsewhere. That is a very defeating mindset and we need to move past that with a pace faster than that of light.

Molemo was inundated with offers of study support at an institution of his choice. After careful thought and thorough consultation with an array of stakeholders including his Mathematics teacher and his parents, he made up his mind and went to the University of Cape Town to pursue studies in Mechanical Engineering. He signed up with three companies for payment of his fees, accommodation and allowances for his upkeep. With the finances out of the way, it was unclear why he appeared to be uncomfortable.

It emerged upon enquiry that his anxiety arose from the reality that he will for the very first time be spending a lot of time on his own and in foreign territory. It was not a confirmed fear of being on his own per se which is known as autophobia or monophobia but thoughts which were building up based on his circumstances. We should not forget that he has never been out of Pretoria for more than three days at a time. He has never set foot in the Mother City or any other province except for Limpopo.

Besides the once off visit to Mbilwi Secondary School a few years earlier, during the December holidays Molemo and his siblings would spend time in rural Ntwane next to Dennilton. Ntwane was about an hour and half away from Mamelodi, it was literally in proximity. He derived great pleasure from the uncomplicated approach most of the residents of the area had to life. Even in this era of technological advancement, they still spend time at the local leader's kraal known as Kgorong in Mmametje. The rich stories of the Bantwane people are still shared through oral tradition. One of these stories as fondly narrated by the elders is that they moved from Botswana before they finally settled in Ntwane. They had to fend off anyone they came across as it was common in those days.

Sometimes there was a need for them to defend themselves from tribes who would attack them with the view to confiscating their valuables. On other occasions they would have to be on the offensive, attacking other tribes they came across with intent to dispossess them of their wealth. It is from these numerous fights that they earned themselves the name ba Ntwana which loosely translated means the fighters. It is always interesting to listen to the elders relating tales of their mighty kings; the likes of Ramasedi and Mohlamme Mathebe.

Further anxiety arose from not knowing how he would handle his first flight ever. He will be on his own as the flight costs were quite steep and neither his mom, dad nor anyone else for that matter from within his support structures could afford to accompany him. Not that any of them were on a flight before. He was going to be the very first one from all the generations in his family to board a flight. History is going to be made on the 11th January at 8h15. "Would I represent my family well or freak out on the flight?" he wondered. So many questions crossed his mind, but he kept all of them to himself. He was all packed and ready to leave for the Mother City. He had all he needed and more, his mother had ensured that all the items on her checklist were ticked and added a little extra items just in case.

He arrived at O.R. Tambo airport a good three hours ahead of his departure time just in case there were hindrances on the road. Luckily for them there was no hindrance whatsoever. They had plenty of time to have his bags checked in, have breakfast and say their goodbyes. He admired the synergy with which the ground staff at the airport operated and felt less anxious about some of the concerns he had earlier on.

The family's parting was not as good as anticipated, it was a very teary affair. None of the family members spoke about their concerns and or anxieties but their eyes welled unceremoniously. The tears rolled effortlessly from each of them that you could have sworn that they were hit by a huge calamity. When boarding announcements were made, they all realised that they should allow Molemo to join his fellow travelers on the other side. As he left them, he resembled the satellite figure wrenched from its orbit, that go drifting away as referred to by Cecil Day Lewis in his poem "Walking Away."

> It is eighteen years ago, almost to the day –
> A sunny day with leaves just turning,
> The touch-lines new-ruled – since I watched you play
> Your first game of football, then, like a satellite
> Wrenched from its orbit, go drifting away
> Behind a scatter of boys. I can see
> You walking away from me towards the school
> With the pathos of a half-fledged thing set free
> Into a wilderness, the gait of one
> Who finds no path where the path should be?
> That hesitant figure, eddying away
> Like a winged seed loosened from its parent stem,
> Has something I never quite grasp to convey
> About nature's give-and-take – the small, the scorching
> Ordeals which fire one's irresolute clay.

I have had worse partings, but none that so
Gnaws at my mind still. Perhaps it is roughly
Saying what God alone could perfectly show –
How selfhood begins with a walking away,
And love is proved in the letting go.

Two hours or so later they had landed in the Mother City. The flight was smooth except for a negligible number of times they experienced turbulence. "Not bad at all, I can do this again soon", he thought. He called home to let them know that they had arrived safely and there was so much more to tell. The jealous airtime cut his intentions very short and he had to proceed with other important things that awaited him and his peers such as finding the keys to the room he would call home for the years he would be spending at the University of Cape Town and attendance of the Orientation at the Engineering and the Built Environment scheduled for later that day.

Molemo was allocated a room at Kilindini residence situated at the corner of Main and Chapel Roads in Rosebank. It had the capacity to house 32 male students in its single rooms. This eased the pressure on Molemo because he could adapt to his new environment with greater ease given the fewer number of students at the residence. Other residences housed in excess of 300 students, so it was indeed a blessing for him to be housed at Kilindini.

He blended in very well with the diverse community at the residence with constant visits to the local pubs. He could not believe the amount of freedom he had. Whether he went to church on Sundays was up to him, attending classes or submitting work was entirely up to him. He spent a lot of time in his room recovering from the escapades of the previous night's hopping from pub to pub in Rosebank, Mowbray and the neighbouring Observatory. These were known student friendly areas and were very accommodating to the pocket as well.

Most of these places did not attract other clientele besides the students due to unpleasantries they would have to go through once the students have had one too many. There would be blissful episodes of laughter from every other corner of the establishment as though there was some competition. Without warning there would be displaced yet passionate chants of the war cries often out of tune yet with extreme energy. This would be unbearable to other patrons who came to the pubs to imbibe their drinks in peace after hectic days at the office.

The summary of result received before the Easter break painted a very sad story of an incapable student who would have to repeat the course the following year. The impressive marks attained at the end of last year are nowhere to be seen. Assignments are not done with the kind of diligence they deserve, and submission is largely for compliance. No wonder the low marks Molemo continues to accrue.

It took a very sobering discussion with one of his peers that he was reminded of the real reasons he was in the Mother City. It was just coincidental because Molemo was asking Benny to join them later that evening at one of the local pubs. He had received his allowance and intended to have a blast with his crew. Drinks on me he gloated. Benny declined the offer politely and went on to explain how much he would struggle to continue with his studies should his scholarship award be withdrawn. He expressed just how lucky he was to have received the offers he had as most of his peers back home in Sehlakwane, Limpopo are struggling to find opportunities.

This jogged Molemo's memory about how similar their challenges were. He did not understand why he was suddenly behaving in the manner he is as this is not in any way in line with his ambition, passion and or upbringing. Post the discussion he vowed to mend his ways. He became a regular visitor at the library and lecture halls. His work ethic had improved considerably and the end of the first semester results confirmed his efforts. He had learnt to prioritise his school work going out occasionally with the few friends he kept. The bulk of the friends decided to ditch him when he gave excuse after another as to why he would not be joining them for drinks.

Some students get too excited once they enjoy the freedom of being on their own. The joy of not having parents looking over and belting out instructions all the time about what you should or should not do, how and why often shifts the focus on the task at hand. These students often return home without the qualifications they went out to get. They regret opportunities they have lost which they cannot unfortunately get back. They regret the recklessness in their behaviour which may have led to failing their studies, unwanted pregnancies, contraction of diseases, withdrawal of financial support and an array of other unsavoury results.

The same fate would have befallen Molemo had he ignored the wake-up call. Without realising, he had become too comfortable trying to fit in and almost lost his identity. He acted out of character often, compromising the very values he stood for. Fortunately, he had turned the corner and saw value in delayed gratification. He knew that he had to do what he needs to do so that he can be able to do what he wants to. It is very important to understand that each of us has a purpose to fulfil. We are not born to follow crowds but to create meaningful paths through which society can traverse on their way to finding their ultimate fulfilment.

Echo Bodine says; 'A lot of people are not comfortable being apart from the group, from the whole herd, and listening to the inner voice. They just follow what the crowd does and wear what the crowd wears and think what the crowd thinks. They get very caught up in doing what the world says is the cool thing to do and living the way the rest of the world lives. Once we make a decision to break away from that and not be part of the herd anymore – by going inside and finding our own voice – then life just becomes magical.'

Do not be afraid to embrace who you are and the purpose you are destined to fulfil. Viktor E Frankl sums it up beautifully in Man's Search for meaning that; 'Everyone has his own specific vocation or mission in life; everyone must carry out a concrete assignment that demands fulfilment. Therein he cannot be replaced, nor can his life be repeated. Thus, everyone's task is unique as is his specific opportunity to implement it.' We are stronger than we think.

CHAPTER 5

"Thousands Of Candles Can Be Lit From A Single Candle, And The Life Of The Candle Will Not Be Shortened." -Buddha

Molemo has returned to the dusty streets of Mamelodi twice already. He has grown very fond of being on the two-hour flights from Gauteng to Cape Town. He regretted taking Benny's advice to take a bus to Gauteng on this one occasion. It was a grueling 18-hour trip in a packed bus with few stops for stretching their legs in between. He swore that he would rather save enough money for flight tickets and never take a bus trip again. It was the long hours and the discomfort of the packed bus that made him swear never to take the bus again, the company and the engaging scenery were mind blowing. Benny possessed wisdom way beyond his age. His discussions with Molemo were quite intriguing. The discussions on the bus were not different either.

An older man sitting next to the two youngsters could not hold back his excitement having eavesdropped on their intense discussions. He commended the young men on their focus as well as the quality of their discussions for the greater part of the trip. 'With young people like yourselves, our country is indeed in good hands!' he exclaimed.

This comment left an indelible mark in the growing minds of Benny and Molemo. They both vowed to strive to contribute in any way possible towards the betterment of those they interact with both in their individual capacity or as part of like-minded groupings. Back in Mamelodi, his home was flooded with teenagers who wanted to know how university life was though many were mostly interested in life in Cape Town – the visits to the many beaches in the Province, trails on seventh wonder of the world (Table mountain), the pleasures of being on his own without constant bother from parents and the exposure to night life on the infamous Long Street.

He always spoke about the huge amount of temptation to steer away from one's goals as a result of all the wonderful destructions the city offered. Emphasising without fail, the need to keep your focus lest you forget the main reason you were in university. He never mentioned his veering off the goals he had set for himself in the first three months of his stay there which almost cost him his multiple scholarship awards. He wanted to maintain his perfect score sheet. He often referred to this one friend of his who was saved by making the Damascus turn. You cannot lie to everyone all the time, some were able to realise that this nameless friend was actually Molemo. They understood that the most important thing in life was not based on never falling but was mostly about rising after every fall.

It came as no surprise as his alma mater, J Kekana High School invited him to speak at their Matric Dance. Three other schools in Pretoria extended their invitation for him to speak after they heard about the quality of his offering.

He did not disappoint at all. The more times he presented, the better his presentations became. The end of the year results confirmed that hard work does pay. He nailed all the courses attaining an average of 75%. He wasn't the best in his cohort, but he was ecstatic about this achievement especially noting the near fall he faced earlier in the year.

He observed the very low marks attained by many students in the Engineering and the Built Environment and spotted an opportunity to help improve their performance while making some money. He spoke to his friend Benny who liked the idea to start tutoring their peers for a fee. Four months later, they had roped in six more of their friends into the tutoring space and they were all smiling all the way to the bank.

The inclusion of other partners was necessitated by their expansion into other faculties. Benny and Molemo as the founding members of this tutoring initiative received money from their partners almost without lifting a finger. Theirs was to check the online requests, assign the tutors to their clients and bill the clients. Their services became quite popular and they were as a result inundated with requests.

The young men's bank balances swelled beyond their wildest expectations. They started skipping the 'boring' meals at the residence and became regular diners at posh restaurants. They were suddenly attracted to the so-called fine things in life. They shopped for famous pricey brands at the Victoria and Alfred centre at the Waterfront. It was very easy for one to mistake them for internationally acclaimed music artists with the bling and glam they always displayed.

Some of the unintended consequences of their sudden success included constant invitations to parties and events attended by the who's who at the University of Cape Town. Their popularity grew with the passing of each day. A lot of students aspired to be like them with some who met them more recently thinking that they have always been part of the shining elites. You and I know the road travelled by these two fortunate youngsters who have just found the proverbial pot of gold at the end of their rainbows. Everything is about them as they seem to have forgotten all about everyone else back home.

The efforts Molemo made during his high school career when he got some money from the helping out learners with learning challenges. He understood the beyond basic needs that he and his siblings had and ensured that when he satisfied his own needs, he satisfied his siblings' needs as well. He continued to spoil them with items of clothing and money.

The second-year curriculum was conquered somewhat effortlessly looking from afar. It was not as easy as it looked as the young men had to juggle a number of balls and ensured that all remained in the air. It was not possible to do so all the time and whenever some balls were dropped, they had to come up with measures to redress that situation. When Molemo went back home for the end of the year break, he felt different. The place felt very foreign, very slow for his liking. The youngsters who came to visit him were in awe as he related tales of elegance and the fine things in life. Food at acclaimed fancy restaurants, pricey 'respected' clothing brands, attendance of functions graced by the elites and being generally in the limelight. His Instagram account confirmed that he was a formidable force with a following in excess of 290 000. He said very little about the academics or lifestyle challenges which earned him the slots to speak at last year's Matric dances and a place in the hearts of aspirant learners and their hopeful parents. His peers from Mamelodi avoided him like a plague as they felt he was out of their league.

His siblings had a better understanding of what he meant as he had introduced them to this life of luxury. He would from time to time bring them expensive brands of clothing and sneakers. On other occasions, he would take them to Sandton City where they would choose what they wanted, and he would gladly foot the bill. They would then visit some of the fine restaurants such as Café Della Salute, Funtastica, Pigalles, Parca Ferme, JB's Corner, Trumps Grillhouse and The Butcher to name but a few.

His father's constant advice that he uses money sparingly fell on deaf ears. I am sure that had he heeded the call to save his earnings and not spend money as if it was about to expire, he would by now be boasting an enviable chunk of savings. He bought a lot of groceries too whenever he was home, making each of his visits memorable especially to his siblings. Buying groceries was something his father was completely against. He felt that it was his responsibility to provide for his family and needed no assistance in that department. He was also against sheer extravagance displayed by Molemo which in his view was not sustainable. He did not want his family to be exposed to things they did not necessarily need.

His insistence on the purchase of basic groceries could not be sufficiently emphasized. You could not miss the glow on Molemo's mom's face which was induced by a sense of pride on seeing how his eldest child has transformed into this young responsible adult. She was indeed the envy of many mothers in this community. You would often hear some mothers urging their charges to spend time with Molemo and learn how he managed to strengthen and sustain his financial muscle. Others could be heard scolding their children labelling them 'good for nothing' as they were outclassed by a small child. They too should take a leaf out of Molemo's book and emulate his movement up the rungs of this ladder called life.

It is interesting to note that most members of any society expect everyone to peak at the same time. If one person gets something right, then everyone else should be able to do so with little or no difficulty. We tend to forget that each of us has a purpose to fulfil and that there are for some valid reasons timelines set for the fulfilment of each of our purposes. Methinks life would be such a bore if everyone achieved everything at the same time with the application of the same effort. It is for this reason that I think that every person should be allowed to shine when they are physically and mentally ready to do so and not when society expects them to do so.

The Afrikaans saying that; 'Die agter os kom ook in die kraal.' (Loosely translated it means that the ox that lags behind will eventually reach its kraal) sums up the unique nature of our journeys. No two children learn to crawl, speak or walk at the same time despite receiving the same quality of support and upbringing.

We should therefore allow, nurture and support everyone to mature and peak according to their levels of readiness. I found the following post by Hakeem Shah quite intriguing:

Obama retired at 55, Trump started at 70. Sydney is 3 hours ahead of Perth, but that doesn't make Perth slow. Someone graduated at the age of 22 but waited 5 years before securing a good job. Someone became a CEO at 25 and died at 50. While another became a CEO at 50 and lived to 90 years.

Someone is still single, while someone else got married. Everyone in this world works based on their time zone. People around you might seem to be ahead of you and some might seem to be behind you. But everyone is running their own race, in their own time. Do not envy them and do not mock them. They are in their time zone, and you are in yours. Life is about waiting for the right moment to act. So, relax, you're not early. You're not late. You are very much on time.

Whatever it is that you are pursuing, do not lose hope of achieving it. Keep the faith that it will manifest eventually. Whatever goals you aspire to achieve are still within your reach, believe me when I say that they can be achieved. Keep the focus and exert the required effort and victory is certain. Neal A Maxwell sums it up beautifully through the quote; "Faith in God includes faith in His timing." For fear of digressing and losing my chain of thought, let me leave this discussion on purpose and the fulfilment thereof for another day. Your thoughts?

CHAPTER 6

"Every Sunset Brings The Promise Of A New Dawn." - Ralph Waldo Emerson

Contrary to fears of possible challenges arising from the intensity of studies, the tutoring partnership went unhindered in Molemo's final year of study. I must add that it was not as easy as it were in the second and third year but Molemo and his partner Benny as well as those in their employ ensured that they delivered their services with excellence while maintaining excellence in the execution of their schoolwork. Money kept on piling into their accounts funding their lavish lifestyles.

The visit by prospective employers at the University of Cape Town served as a constant reminder that their time at the institution was about to end. Molemo attended all presentations by these company representatives and completed almost all application forms for potential employment with the belief that he should not place all his eggs in one basket. He would rather be inundated with multiple opportunities and decide on the one he deems more suitable to pursue. Some of Molemo's peers were intending to further their studies beyond the bachelor's degree which seemed to be more within their grasp.

He had for time without number made attempts to twist his parents' arms into allowing him to pursue an Honours and a Master's degree before seeking employment but his requests fell on deaf ears. They would not have any of it. All they wanted was for him to start work with the hope that the quality of their lives would change for the better. They assumed that there would be a third and very decent income in the household which would remove most if not all their financial woes. I cannot blame them for thinking in this manner given the kind of responsibility Molemo had displayed through his ample generosity. Do you think he would be returning home to his parents and continuing to live with them after spending four years as an independent young man?

The final year was as good as done and dusted. Celebrations of friendships started on campus were the order of each day. Many a student committing to maintain contact and sustain the great relationships they have started. Most of these were based on their current understanding of reality and none of them considered the potential challenges of the world of work. The expected focus on what one is hired to perform for at least eight hours of every day could be quite daunting. The pursuit of new relationships and continuation of some which were started at varsity posed another challenge to those who have just joined the world of work. Molemo's family was blown away by their first experience of the Mother City. They flew in two days before the graduation so that they could visit some of the tourist attraction points. His father was particularly interested in setting foot on the iconic Robben Island where many African leaders spent considerable time behind bars.

They got onto the ferry with great enthusiasm, not so long ago they were in an airplane and now on a boat! They could not hide their excitement and the many selfies they took on the ferry was proof of their exhilaration. On their arrival they were met by friendly tour guides most of them were imprisoned on the notorious island. Many of the stories they shared was from their personal experiences and not what they read or heard from someone else.

The strong themes that emerged from the tour guides were that of resilience and determination. A pure display of tough and unbreakable spirits. The narration of the conditions of the incarceration of Robert Mangaliso Sobukwe left many a tourist teary. It was unthinkable that a person would be held in solitary confinement even after completing his sentence. He is said to have been denied opportunity to converse with others on the island as the authorities at the time feared that he would influence them to remain resolute in their commitment to overthrow the government of that time. He would from time to time when he went out of his house on the island to exercise, use hand gestures to communicate with his comrades. He would pick a handful of soil, raise his right arm and release the soil. This gesture was interpreted as 'izwe lethu' or 'umhlaba wethu' meaning this is our land. A rapturous response of 'iAfrica!' would reverberate across the island.

Another interesting development shared by the former prisoners who served as guides was the robust nature of debates that happened of the island. These were across the ideological homes of the prisoners with each defending their approach towards the struggle for the freedom of the African majority in

South Africa. Most prisoners emerged from the island as graduates having ensured that they equip themselves with knowledge and skills and not just lament the negative aspects of being imprisoned. The father of our nation, Nelson Mandela is one such leader who ensured that he furthered his studies while imprisoned on the island. Anthony Sampson, the British writer and journalist also known for Mandela the authorised Biography, referred to Robben Island as the island that schooled a generation of leaders. Many credible leaders spent time on the island as political prisoners.

The family's first day in Cape Town went faster than they had anticipated. It was dark before they could complete all they wanted to, and they had to retreat to their temporary self-catering home in Bellville. Everyone had something to say about their experiences. These ranged from the flight they took in the morning coming to Cape Town, the ride in the ferry to Robben Island, the narrations by the former political prisoners, the brutality of the apartheid government, the lunch enjoyed at the Victoria and Alfred Waterfront, the aerial cableway and the amazing experience of the sunset on Table Mountain. The youngsters could not wait for an opportunity to brag to their peers and educators through the essays they would be writing about these experiences.

The next day was equally fun-filled and jam packed. They were on the open top bus to explore the interesting attractions Cape Town had to offer. The tour included a drive to Cape Point, a place alleged to be where the Indian and Atlantic Ocean meet. It is officially reported that the two oceans actually meet at Cape Agulhas.

The most common misunderstanding behind the controversy is the erroneous assumption that oceans and currents are synonymous.

Cape Point- Western Cape

The residents of Cape Agulhas are said to be seething with anger at the loss of potential revenue generating opportunities due to tourists flocking Cape Point instead of their town. Other attractions lined for the day included a visit to the Two Oceans Aquarium and the much-anticipated trip to Mzoli's in Gugulethu. The Two Oceans Aquarium offered opportunities for scuba diving to novice and to experienced professional divers. Those who have been there say that they would not trade their experiences for anything. They explain it as being one with nature or being up close and personal with Mother Nature. This arises from the unique underwater experience close to turtles, rays and guitarfish to name but a few. There is an opportunity to spend time with penguins under the guidance of a bird keeper.

These feathered friends are a marvel to watch as they behave like they would in their natural habitat. Lucky visitors may find a few of these birds hopping onto their laps thereby enhancing their experience. The visit to Mzoli's in Gugulethu is the cherry on top. Molemo's parents have heard their friends saying amazing things about the exhilarating experiences they had at the humble Tshisa Nyama. The plastic chairs and tables as well as the tin plates are in stark contrast to the fanfare displayed at the Victoria and Alfred restaurants. The beautiful and clear view presented through the windows of these strategically built restaurants are completely different from the thick bellowing smoke from the braai. The distinct smell of Mzoli's special secret sauce leaves many a patron drooling. Rumour has it that Mzoli refused offers of loads of cash from both local and international patrons in exchange of the recipe for this secret sauce which doubles as marinate.

Molemo's crew could not believe their eyes when they arrived. The large number of elegant and ordinary cars snaking into Gugulethu, the diverse groups of revelers from different backgrounds, cultures and countries as well as the festive mood suggested that it was an official public holiday even though it was a normal working day in the middle of the week. The family had a ball in Gugulethu with the elders imbibing ice cold alcoholic beverages and the children enjoying their soft drinks. The joyful electrifying and vibey atmosphere arose from a combination of tunes blasting from the DJ's system, the celebratory mood of the patrons and the fulfilment of finally gracing the much revered Tshisa Nyama.

Everyone was up very early the next morning readying themselves for the graduation ceremony. It is the first graduation experienced by Molemo's family in its entirety. None from the family including distant relatives had completed tertiary studies. This increased the level of anticipation, curiosity and excitement. Approximately two and a half hours later chants, praises and ululations congratulating the graduates had subsided. Clicks of camera's and bright broad smiles entrenched deeply the joy brought by the events which unfolded earlier during the graduation ceremony. It is interesting how people get inspired to pursue further study whenever they attend graduation ceremonies. For some it becomes genuine inspiration which they convert into action. They would register courses they would like to complete and fulfil all the requirements. For others it is a momentary inspiration whose momentum fades with time.

The Cape Town visit was on the lips of Molemo's family. They repeatedly narrated their experiences to everyone who cared to listen. There was literally no other topic to share other than their expedition to the Mother City. It has even overshadowed their evident grief at Molemo's decision not to stay with them upon commencing his contract with the power utility Eskom. Though he was based at their head office in Megawatt Park just outside Pretoria, he opted to rent an apartment in Midrand instead of traveling from Mamelodi on a daily basis. Numerous attempts from his parents and everyone who tried to offer their advice fell on deaf ears. He was not going to reverse the gains he has made in the past four years staying on his own in the Western Cape.

He did not see his movements and whereabouts being constantly monitored and somewhat controlled by his parents. He promised to make monthly contributions towards the family's financial wellness as it seemed to be one of the major bones of contention. Remember that uncommunicated expectation of financial relief we expressed earlier? Yes, that very one! Two meagre incomes combined with Molemo's solid third income. The household would have been able to do wonders with the addition of a credible portion of the twenty-two thousand-rand Molemo took home on a monthly basis. He had severed ties with the extra tuition company due to the distance between the Western Cape and Gauteng and the fact that he wanted to give his work all his attention added more substance to the decision. This meant that he had to rely solely on his salary.

One thing he was not aware of was the interest money lenders had on brand new graduates and employees. He too was inundated with offers to take up credit facilities from many companies. The barrage of offers he received from major banks for credit and other related facilities were accepted without careful consideration. He had a card from almost every major bank and hopped happily from one credit facility to another. Molemo's two-bedroom apartment was fully furnished within the first month of occupation. His taste for good things was as clear as daylight. The bulk of what he 'owned' represented exclusivity. Sadly, most of the goods were acquired on credit. His apartment modelled the ideal space people his age and older aspired to acquire. It represented goal attainment and absolute fulfilment to his age group and a few more from other generations of admirers.

Cross generational appreciation it is called. You might be wondering how people across generations knew about the exclusivity of his apartment. Some really outstanding parties spoken of for days on end were hosted in this apartment. When Molemo and his friends hosted parties, they stopped at nothing. You attend one of these parties and you don't want to miss any other. Despite the occasional disturbance by law enforcement officers responding to resident complaints about noise levels, these celebrations were very joyous. New friends outside the varsity space were added. This meant that their activities were not limited to Gauteng. They went everywhere members of the crew and their acquaintances needed their attention.

It was also interesting to note that they would for instance leave for Bloemfontein in the Free state on a Friday afternoon in a convoy of high revving and sound blasting Golf GTI's, BMW's and Mercedes Benzes. They would reach their destination in the evening and party into the wee hours of the next morning going to their booked accommodation around five am. What a waste of the beautiful and luxurious accommodation meant to settle minds and refresh bodies. I would definitely visit these places if I could afford whenever I needed to recharge.

After the usual champagne breakfast, the crew would head back to Johannesburg to prepare for yet another blast of a party. Events, parties and any other excuse to wine, dine and dance characterised each of their weekends. To enhance their social relevance, the crew steered away from humble minimal purse denting beverages to very loud purse banging drinks. Belvedere imported vodka, Veuve Clicquot, Remy Martin VSOP,

Glenfiddich 15-year-old and above, Corona and Grolsch swing top beer would signal their presence at any event. The number of followers on their Instagram accounts bore testimony to the kind and extent of support they had. They posted pictures of almost everything they had or did. Food, beverages, items of clothing, parties attended, upcoming events and even destinations they visited were captured through the fanciest and priciest of gadgets.

It is generally assumed that the pricier things are, the more value they carry. I am sure that there are some credible arguments affirming and opposing this notion. It must, however, be pointed that in the eyes of the majority of our young people who view life through the lens of the influential social media success is measured through the kind of beverage you imbibe, the label of the clothes on your back, the price of the food you eat coupled with the restaurants you frequent, the destinations you visit as well as how you flaunt all these. It is not surprising that some of us will stop at nothing to create an impression of having it all when the truth is, we are struggling and living way below the breadline.

I was disturbed to learn about a young man who decided to buy an elegant car which was way beyond his means. The monthly repayments required that he vacates the apartment he rented, terminate his membership of the medical scheme and stop supporting his siblings back home. The car afforded him the opportunity to be admired and held in high regard. The trick being that no one else knew about his real challenges. He strategically continued with his gym membership because he could maintain the network of acquaintances and grab the attention of those who would be drawn towards him through the car he drove. These were just minor reasons for holding on to the membership, he would be there most mornings when the gym opened to take a decent bath before going to work. His clothes were neatly packed in the boot. Whenever he ran out of friends who could invite him to their homes for the night, he would spend most of his time at waterholes leaving for a nearby filling station to catch a nap. He always ensured that none of his so-called friends had left when he 'called it a night'.

Knowing this young man, I truly wish he had stayed true to himself and not create an impression that he was someone he was nowhere close to becoming. I found this quote by an undisclosed source to be quite profound; 'Don't educate your children to be rich. Educate your children to be happy so that they can appreciate the value of things and not just their price'. Hopefully Molemo and his friends were not affected by the need to appear solid in the eyes of those around them and the massive followers they have attracted on social media. It would be difficult to conclude whether any of the friends was affected by the statement above as each had a unique background.

Some of the guys continued to receive allowances from their folks despite having commenced their roles in the employment sector. They had no real use for the salaries they earned and could do as they pleased with it. On the other hand, Molemo and a few of his peers knew that every cent counted but quickly forgot this very crucial aspect of reality every time an invitation to an event was received. Molemo hoped for some kind of miracle as his available funds continued to dwindle. Life in the fast lane meant almost everything for these young people. They had this fear of missing out. It has been eight months since Molemo made a financial contribution towards the expenses associated with his family. He had stopped contacting any of his siblings because he felt they were putting undue pressure on him with requests for this or that every time he made contact. The animal he had created back when he was in varsity has developed into a monster he cannot domesticate. He can no longer afford to buy the pricey renowned labels for himself and include his siblings as well. He chose to maintain his own lifestyle lest the world looks at him differently.

He could not say no to any of the invitations for more credit. I am sure that there was no facility he did not have. Credit cards from all major banks as well as from those emerging financial institutions, personal loans and those purported to consolidate one's debts. Consolidation after consolidation became the new order. He juggled around robbing Peter in order to pay Paul. He would use a Nedbank credit card in order to pay a Standard Bank credit card he intended to use for the month. This became his modus operandi and unfortunately it was not sustainable. Someday his antics will catch up with him. Molemo maintained his social media life as if all was well in his paradise. He kept posting those blissful moments of splashing cash as if it were going out of fashion much to the admiration of his followers. So many aspired to be like him even if it could be for just a day.

CHAPTER 7

"If You Get Up One More Time Than You Fall, You Will Make It Through." -Tiny Buddha

Molemo has been missing in action from social media for the past two years or so. Attempt to locate him at his flat drew a blank as well. I was actually shocked to learn that he had to leave the flat in a huff to avoid meeting his landlord who was tired of the multiple excuses he gave for non-payment. I was told that he was three months behind on his rental when he left the property. For two months he literally lived on two minute noodles as anything else was expensive. Whenever he found an excuse to go home he went. His main excuse was that he was tired of take-aways and preferred home cooked food. He would often speak highly of his mother's cooking and for that he would be given more food to take back to his apartment when he left.

He has retreated into obscurity, forsaking the glitz and glamour. The proverbial prodigal son has gone back to Mamelodi living with his family. Unlike many of us, he managed to swallow his pride and saw value in going back home and rebuilding his life. Failure is not in falling down but in staying down after a fall, they say.

Molemo was lucky to acknowledge this truth. Many a time and oft we hope for some miracle to happen to save us from the inevitable. We end up getting deeper and deeper into debt to a point of no return. Some of us end up suffering from anxiety and depression as a result of having exhausted all remedial avenues. Many young people with potential for greatness end up succumbing to pressure and taking their lives as a result of their inability to reverse the challenges created by debt and living in and for the limelight. When the tables turn, they just cannot go on without acknowledgement, affirmation and envy of those around them.

I wish we could realise that simple deeds of random kindness which do not require material or financial means can genuinely win the hearts of those around us. Like an old eagle recognising its weakness he retreated back home plucked his feathers, renewed his beak and claws and waited patiently for new ones to develop. During this time he made every effort not to luxuriate, his main objective was to pay back every cent he owed. He understood that by doing so he would regain his freedom from debt and restart life on a new slate. He hardly bought anything he did not need only the essentials.

It seems as though he is turning the corner given the discussion he had with his father about buying a second hand Toyota Tazz. It is nothing compared to the flashy Golf GTI he drove but the difference this time around is that he will be buying it for cash. He has managed to save up some money after paying off his debts. He has regained his voice as well as he has begun to narrate his life journey with great enthusiasm and passion showing clear signs of growth and learning from his experience. The pain of loss of respect and lost opportunities to positively impact the lives of those aspiring youngsters from his community and beyond seems to be have faded with time. He is now determined to alert them about the potential dangers of dependency on credit.

He speaks of how he was blinded by being in the spotlight for all the wrong reasons. He spent money he did not have as the bulk of it was from the many credit cards and loans he had. Extended access to credit delayed his wake up call. Only when he realised that he has run out of options did it dawn on him that he has messed up big time. He came up with every excuse possible whenever his friends wanted to hook up as he could no longer afford their kind of lifestyle. He cautioned that not everyone would be as lucky as he was for a few reasons.

Not everyone would have a chance to go back to a home where there would be less expectations of support from the young people who messed up. The issue of Black tax is not an illusion. Young professionals are expected to support their siblings and other family members who are less fortunate. The wrath of the community may be too overwhelming to handle thereby halting any hope of starting afresh. Inability to handle the 'fall from grace' may signal a dead end for the affected youngster(s) and kill the will to soldier on.

www.ingramcontent.com/pod-product-compliance
Lightning Source LLC
La Vergne TN
LVHW010542100826
845148LV00013B/2568
* 9 7 8 0 6 2 0 9 3 1 0 2 1 *